SARAH
NOT FORSAKEN

Mrs. Silas Bowman

SARAH
NOT FORSAKEN

Mrs. Silas Bowman

Ridgeway Publishing
Medina, New York

SARAH, NOT FORSAKEN

Sarah, Not Forsaken is based on *Sarah Whitcher's Story*
by Elizabeth Yates. Copyright 1994 by BJU Press.
Printed by permission of BJU Press.

*To obtain additional copies
please visit your local
bookstore or contact:*

**Ridgeway Publishing
3129 Fruit Avenue
Medina, NY 14103
toll free: (888) 822-7894
fax: (585) 798-9016**

*Text illustrations by Laura Yoder
Cover illustration by Amanda Yoder*

ISBN# 978-0-9848888-3-2

Printed in the United States of America

A narrative poem telling the true account of the Whitcher family's experience of losing their little daughter, Sarah, in the mountains. After many prayers and days of desperate searching, God worked a miracle that finally ended their nightmare. A faith-building story!

Chapter One

At home in the Whitchers' log cabin

    That nestled in the wooded Pine Hill,

The dinner that Sunday was over,

    The axe and the hammer were still.

And Pa, having read them the story

    Of Job from the Bible that day,

Took Ma by the arm for a visit

    Up Summit, an afternoon stay.

They left, to the children assigning

    The charge of the fire and farm,

And warned that the older be careful

    In keeping the younger from harm.

Young Sarah was neither a baby

    Nor old enough fully to share

The duties that Pa had requested;

    She'd neither a goal nor a care.

With brothers absorbed in their playing,

    Her sister, with Baby's loud wails,

She strayed from the cabin; play-acting

    Like Pa, she traversed forest trails.

Far down from the cabin, she wandered

And waded across Berry Brook,

Then slipped through the towering pine trees,

With neither a thought nor a look,

Until she stepped into a clearing

Where grasses and flowers grew fair.

Delighted, she sat down to gather

The strawberries ripening there.

How sweet in her hunger they tasted!

How gladly she'd take some to Ma—

So suddenly Sarah remembered

Her mother, her home, and her Pa.

Her father would like this wild meadow

For cattle to graze in and rest;

Her Ma would enjoy all the flowers

And strawberries, surely the best.

Now quickly she'd run home to tell them!

But dusk settled, dimming her sight,

And clouds in the west threatened rainfall

And darkening gray of the night.

She darted from out of the clearing.

The forest was dark! On she sped.

The wind in the pine trees a-sighing

She heard, and still faster she fled.

She ran, with her senses all straining:

Where *was* Berry Brook? Where <u>was</u> Pa?

She saw naught and heard naught to guide her

To home and her siblings and Ma.

She ran, and her heart pounded faster

Till, gasping, she stopped in her flight.

She shouted. "Oh, Pa!" she repeated.

But rainfall began with the night.

Chapter Two

Back home in the Whitchers' log cabin,

The children all waited to hear

The shout of their father announcing

That he and their mother were near.

"Where's Sarah?" young Reuben inquired

On seeing that two, and not three,

Came down from the Summit that evening.

"At home she's expected to be,"

Said Pa. "But she's not!" Joseph answered.

"She hasn't been here half the day!"

And John, with great shock, recollected

He never had watched her in play!

"She's lost!" Ma exclaimed in quick anguish.

But Pa, though his features were drawn,

Replied, "If she's lost, we will find her.

She'll surely be home before dawn.

"Trust God," Pa reminded the mother.

"Like Job, always trust in the Lord."

And Ma, though bereft, held the promise,

The peace that this hope could afford.

Pa hastily left with the lantern.

He searched all along Berry Brook—

The places that Sarah would venture,

Each pool, and each sheltering nook.

Young Reuben blew loud with the bugle;

The echoes in circling "haloo's"

Called out from their cabins the settlers,

Who hurried to hear of the news.

Nine men in an hour had gathered

To help in the search for the child.

With lanterns and horns, they assembled,

And down from Pine Hill they all filed.

They called for the wandering Sarah,

They searched under thickets and trees,

They checked every boulder. Would Sarah

Have curled up to sleep among these?

At home Ma began a bright fire,

    The boys gathered wood for the blaze,

In hopes that their wandering sister

    Would notice its beckoning rays.

Night deepened. All came to the cabin.

Men told of the trails they forsook,

How some of them went to the boulder

That lies well beyond Berry Brook.

"She couldn't have gone all that distance!"

Said one. But the next said, "She might.

That boulder, though, shelters a varmint,

She wouldn't stay there for a night."

And so the talk spun round the fire;

    Each failure man blamed on the dark.

Then Pa said, "Clear skies for the morrow

    Give hope for a sign or a mark."

Each man as he shouldered his weapon

    And strode down the path in the night

Spoke words of support to the mother:

    "We'll come with the breaking of light."

That night, Ma the fire attended

    While Pa and the children all slept.

With thoughts of her Sarah in danger. . .

    Alone. . . in the darkness. . . Ma wept.

Then yearning for morning, she added

    More wood to refuel the ray,

Its light giving hope and thus hastening

    The coming return of the day.

The news of lost Sarah had traveled

All over the county, and men

Came tramping by scores into Warren

To search for the infant again.

So Pa led some men through the maples

To Black Brook and past Kelly Pond,

But none saw a clue or a footprint

Beside all the path or beyond.

Then up the long climb past the Oak Falls,

The men labored up the divide;

They reached Wachipauka's deep water

That lies there beneath Webster's Slide.

And there on the lakeshore they shouted,

Though worn from the grueling job.

But the mountain protected its secret

And gave but an echoing sob.

"Where now?" asked the men of Pa Whitcher,

Their hopes for success ebbing low.

"Why, back to Pine Hill," he gave answer,

"Still searching wherever we go."

All up Oliverian River,

    Some searched, looking into each pool,

And thought how a child in her playing

    Might stop for a drink, fresh and cool,

Then falling, plunge into the current. . .

    But none saw a sign or a trace,

Although to the source of the river

    They searched every possible place.

At sundown, all met at the cabin

To eat from the simmering stew

That Ma ladled out from the cauldron;

Yet none could report any clue.

Each man, as he left, turned to Mother

To offer what comfort he might:

"I'm sorry we still haven't found her.

I'll come with the first morning light."

"Our Sarah's so small!" Ma wept wildly.

"At night— oh, she'll come to some harm!"

"She's big for her age," Pa responded,

Attempting to still her alarm.

"My wife, every man in the county

Is doing the best that he can

To help in the search for our Sarah.

The Lord, He will help every man."

Next morning the searchers had doubled;

The news had swept valley and glen.

And over the mountains and rivers,

On horseback, on foot, came the men.

Pa welcomed them all and gave orders:

They'd split into companies now

And follow the point of the compass;

Through deepest of forest they'd plow.

They'd search every place they had covered;

Again they would comb every nook.

At intervals calling each other,

They'd carefully, doggedly look!

Three short and sharp blasts with the bugle

Would signal that Sarah was found.

So off they went, tramping through forest,

Though strange and uneven the ground.

They went. But their ears that were listening

And craving to hear the glad cry—

The welcoming blast of the bugle—

Went hungry as hours crept by.

At sunset they gathered for supper

Beside the same cabin again.

The final man dashed down the ridges

With a message that startled the men.

"Ho! Footprints!" he shouted. "I saw them!

Her footprints were there in the sand

Beside Berry Brook, and they weren't

A mile from the place where we stand!"

"Footprints?" gasped Pa. "Were they small ones?"

The messenger nodded his head,

Then added, "Beside them were paw prints—

A bear's!" And each heart filled with dread.

The man splayed his hand, and he pressed it

To earth to show something of size.

None spoke, and the frightening silence

Did eloquently tell the heart cries.

"She's torn into pieces!" one murmured.

"All eaten!" another agreed.

Ma covered her face with her apron;

The children drew near in their need.

"It may be a she-bear," said Uncle.

"If so, like as not, she's unharmed."

In silence they swallowed their supper

Though many were truly alarmed.

The next day was just like the others:

They started with hope running high,

For surely today they would find her

Somewhere near the brook that ran by!

They searched, but in vain! Nothing further

Appeared to their hungering eyes.

The sun set behind the dark mountains

Without their attaining the prize.

"We never will find her," they murmured;

Despairing and weary, they went.

Pa thanked them for all of their efforts,

For all of the time they had spent.

But Ma, when she saw they were leaving,

Forsaking the child she adored,

Ran onto the path, arms extended;

For Sarah once more she implored.

"Kind neighbors, kind friends, former strangers,"

She pleaded with tone low and mild,

"For love that you bear your own infants,

Please, search one more day for our child."

Ma faced them; her arms she hung limply.

She waited. The men looked away

And then at each other. They nodded.

"We'll come to your aid one more day."

"God bless you!" Ma whispered as meekly

They passed her and left, one by one.

Then sobbing, she crumpled together

And prayed as she never had done.

"You're asking too much," Pa admonished.

"They each have their work to attend."

But still, relief shone in his features

To think of the hope they would lend.

Chapter Three

When Sarah, that Sunday, heard rainfall,

She knew she must find for the night

Some shelter, some place for protection.

And soon there appeared to her sight

A little ahead in the darkness

What looked like a cabin of stone.

No door could she find there, but only

A hollow to crawl in alone.

She rested awhile on the leaf bed,

Then out in the darkness she crept.

She thought, as she leaned on the boulder,

Would Pa find her here while she slept?

She called for her pa, but no answer.

Instead, far away in the night,

She heard Berry Brook gaily babbling

And knew Pa would come with a light.

A dark shape came moving toward her,

    She wondered just what it could be;

And then in an instant she knew it—

    "Oh, Ollie! You're coming for me!"

She shouted with joy for her playmate;

    But what a big dog he was now!

She felt quite afraid, but decided

    At night all was different, somehow.

Still closer he came with a snuffling,

    And Sarah stepped slowly quite near.

Indeed, he was too big to hug him,

    And, oh, but the smell was so queer!

He started to lick at her scratches;

    Then all her doubts melted away.

She stroked his rough head with her fingers

    As often she'd done in her play.

She showed him her bouquet of flowers.

But then to her utter surprise,

He ate them all up in a hurry!

She couldn't believe her own eyes!

Why Ollie! He'd never eat flowers!

What made him so suddenly queer?

"Oh, Ollie, please take me home quickly!"

She begged, overcome with new fear.

Instead he bumped hard against Sarah.

Though puzzled, she felt she must do

Whatever her Ollie decided,

Though all was so strange and so new.

He nuzzled her into the hollow

And followed her into his den.

She burrowed her head in his bosom

And nestled right up against him.

He swatted her into position

And held her tight close to his side,

And then came the sound she remembered—

The comforting hum from inside.

The sound made her feel very sleepy,

The same as when Ma sang a song.

But, oh! She must pray before sleeping;

Forgetting would surely be wrong.

She tried to get up, but her Ollie

Still tighter held her in embrace;

And so she prayed where she was lying,

Though truly she felt out of place.

She slept then, exhausted from walking,

  Not knowing that late in the night

Two men met beside the big boulder

  To talk in their lantern's dim light.

One stopped in mid-sentence to listen.

  "You hear what a noise that bear makes?"

"I do," said the other, "and wouldn't

  Feel safe to be here when he wakes."

They passed on, still searching for Sarah,

  Not guessing how near Sarah lay.

Protected and warmed by the varmint,

  She slept until breaking of day.

She woke and saw Ollie had left her.

So sorry that she was too late,

She looked out to see him just leaving.

"Oh, Ollie!" she shouted. "Please wait!"

Surprised that her dog didn't listen,

She thought then he'd gone to find Pa

To bring him to her, so he'd carry

Her safely back home to her ma.

She settled back down in the hollow

   Where soon she was sleeping again.

When later she woke, the bright sunlight

   Was shining on her in the den.

She crawled out. And feeling quite hungry,

   She wished for more strawberries sweet.

Would Ollie be able to find her

   Out looking for something to eat?

"I'd better not go," she decided.

   Instead, from low branches she ate

The tender new tips of the hemlock,

   Then sat by the boulder to wait.

While playing with twigs, she heard voices;

The blowing of horns echoed near.

She listened. Was that someone calling?

She shouted, and hoped Pa would hear.

Again and again she called loudly,

But only her echo she heard.

It made her feel queer that none answered;

From then on, she said not a word.

The blowing of horns grew more distant,

The voices all faded away.

It surely was not Sarah Whitcher

The men had been calling today.

When dusk settled over the forest,

    Big Ollie came out of the trees.

She ran to him, hugging him warmly,

    And begged him, "Oh, take me home, please!

"Oh, Ollie, where's Pa? I'm so hungry!"

    But Ollie just pushed her ahead

And thumped her and bumped her and tumbled

    Her into the hollow instead.

Still, she was relieved to see Ollie

    And laughed to be with him again,

But Ollie just hugged her and licked her

    And hummed her to sleep in his den.

The next day was much like the other:

    She followed her friend to the brook,

She drank, and she washed, and she rested,

    And always for food would she look.

When Ollie came back in the evening,

    Young Sarah was eager for play.

But Ollie just firmly embraced her,

    And Sarah then slept until day.

When Sarah saw Ollie had left her

  And still hadn't gone to get Pa,

She knew she must search for their cabin;

  Alone she must find Pa and Ma.

She crawled slowly out of the hollow

  And stood up to start on her way.

She saw that her dress was all dirty

  And torn from her long forest stay.

A brook flowed nearby, but to Sarah

  It seemed much too deep and too wide

To be Berry Brook; but just maybe

  If she walked along by its side,

This water would join with the water

    That made up the real Berry Brook,

And so she could find their own cabin.

    Yes, that was the way she would look.

She drank from the stream, waded in it

    To wash all the dirt from her feet,

Then nibbled on lichens and flowers

    And ferns, to have something to eat.

The warmth of the day made her sleepy;

And as she turned back from the stream,

She stumbled and fell. . . and lay silent

And rested as if in a dream.

When later she searched for some shelter,

She heard once again on the breeze

The far distant echo of voices,

The blowing of horns through the trees.

She'd heard them so often; she fancied

The sounds—sometimes far, sometimes nigh—

Were really a part of the forest,

Like wind sweeping up to the sky.

Her eyes blurred; she stumbled, so-o-o tired.

With effort she crept to a place

Where branches torn off from a pine tree

Created a small, sheltered space.

She snuggled deep under the branches,

All dirty and hungry and worn;

And Ollie came there to protect her,

Slept with her until the next morn.

Chapter Four

On Thursday Ma gave up her station

Of cooking for so many men,

And she and her boys joined the others

To search for their Sarah again.

Kind neighborly women replaced her

In tending the little ones there

And keeping the home fire burning,

The cauldron of beans to prepare.

At noon, after feeding the children,

    They tucked them in bed for a spell,

Then sat down outside near the cabin

    To rest their own bodies as well.

The sounding of horns in the distance

    No longer attracted the ear.

They dozed. . . then they started. What was that?

    What footsteps were treading so near?

A wayfarer entered the clearing,

A youthful one, haggard and worn.

"I've come up from Plymouth," he told them,

And set down the sack he had borne.

"A-foot all those miles? Must be thirty!"

The women in wonderment cried.

"Then where are you bound?" they inquired.

"To find the lost child," he replied.

"Please give me some food and some water;

I've walked all this way without rest.

And after I've eaten a morsel,

I'm off to accomplish my quest."

"You know well these mountains?" they asked him

While filling a noggin to drink.

"I've never been here," he admitted.

"You haven't? Man, what do you think?

"For days now, our men have been searching;

They know all this land as their own.

And you, but a stranger, talk boldly

Of finding the child all alone?"

In spite of their doubting, the women

Still served him a bowl full of beans.

He thanked them and ate; and when finished,

Said, "Let me explain what this means.

"Last night when I came into Plymouth,

(My surname is Heath, by the way)

I heard of a child who had wandered

Far off in the forest one day.

"I prayed that some settler would find her,

And then before midnight, I dreamed.

That I was the person who found her,

Although it preposterous seemed.

"Three times in my dreaming, I saw her

Where branches a shelter had made.

A she-bear was there to protect her,

As resting she lay in a glade.

I dreamed it three times in succession,

And always the path grew more clear;

And now I must hasten to find her

If someone will guide me till near."

Just then from the door of the cabin

   Came Betsey with sleep-laden eyes.

She looked at the wayfaring stranger

   With wonderment, fear, and surprise.

The women both saw that the stranger

   Had started. Then shaking his head,

He said, "First I thought 'tis the same one,

   But, no, for <u>her</u> hair was all red."

And Betsey, now fully awakened,

    Walked bravely right up to the man

And asked, "Will you find my dear sister?"

    "I will, if I possibly can,"

Heath said as he tightened his bootlace;

    Then added, "I'll quickly go forth

If someone will show me directly

    The bridle path off to the north."

Just then Joseph Patch walked toward them,

All worn from the wearisome days

Of searching for little lost Sarah

Through rugged and forested ways.

His wife told him all of Heath's story.

But Joseph, exhausted and weak,

Refused to believe it authentic—

Too tired and troubled to speak.

She held to his arm in deep earnest

And gravely said, "Husband, take heed.

He seems to be humble and honest,

And may prove to be just what we need."

Then Joseph looked long and sincerely

At Heath as he still waited there.

Indeed, Patch was willing for someone

To help them—so deep their despair!

"And so?" Patch confronted the stranger.

Heath spoke. "Tell me where I can look

To find me a path going northward.

That crosses a sizable brook."

"'Tis the Oliverian River,"

    Patch answered. "I well know the place."

With slow, weighted words, Heath continued,

    "A little southeast is a space

Where lies a pine tree that is broken,

    Its top fallen down to the ground.

It forms with its branches a shelter,

    And there the lost child will be found."

Patch nodded and turned from the cabin.

Heath followed; and matching his stride,

Together the ridge-top they mounted

And trudged down the opposite side.

Though tired, they tramped ever northward

And reached Oliverian's bank;

They paused there to rest for a moment,

And from the fresh water they drank.

When on the far side of the river,

Said Patch, "Now it's you who must lead."

"I will," Heath replied, stepping forward,

"If you to my guiding give heed."

Heath stopped to consider a moment;

Then turning, he stepped from the track

And plunged through the thickets and bushes,

Though Patch to him called to come back,

"There's no way through that!" "But it's my way,"

Heath answered, "and I'm going through!"

Then drawn by Heath's confident bearing,

Patch followed to see what he'd do.

Ahead stood a wind-shattered pine tree,

  Its trunk opened up to the sky.

Here Heath pushed his way through the tangle

  To find where the infant should lie.

He looked where the treetop had fallen—

  And there, as the vision had shown,

The child lay in innocent slumber,

  Alive, undisturbed, and alone.

He paused until Patch stood beside him

And gazed at the girl on the ground.

Young Sarah, the Whitchers' lost darling,

Had finally, safely been found!

And Joseph so tenderly lifted

The child from her leaf-littered bed

While Heath shot the gun as a signal

That Sarah was found. . . and not dead!

"Alive! It is true! They have found her!

To God be all glory and praise!"

And so the hills rang with the triumph;

The searchers abandoned their ways.

The message spread quickly and echoed,

And men their fatigue all forgot

In hastening by to see Sarah,

The child they'd so earnestly sought.

When Sarah awoke from her slumber,

She looked at the neighbor she knew,

And murmured, "Please take me to Mama!

I want to go home. Take me, do!"

"I'll take you right home," answered Joseph.

Before they had time to arrive,

The Whitchers all gathered to meet her,

So glad to see Sarah alive!

And Joseph stepped forward with Sarah

And laid her safe into the arm

Of Ma, who so long had been praying

Her darling be kept from all harm.

"Oh, Sarah! My dear little Sarah!"

Ma cried in a torrent of tears,

Releasing the joy and the sorrow,

The strain of her anguish and fears.

Then Pa hugged his Sarah and held her

Up high for the searchers to see.

Her brothers danced round in excitement,

They shouted and chattered with glee.

In silence, Heath stood near the others.

Pa met him and, grasping his hand,

Gazed into the eyes of the stranger—

A look they could both understand.

"I knew that the Lord would do something

To help us and show us His might,"

Said Pa. And a childish voice answered,

"He made everything come out right!"

While all of them walked to the cabin,

Each one was delighted to see

That Sarah looked healthy and happy;

And everyone wanted to be

Close by her, to touch her and see her,

And everyone wanted to hear

What happened while she had been missing;

And hadn't she felt any fear?

To everyone, Sarah gave answer:

"My Ollie came to me each night.

He warmed me and stayed close beside me

And guarded me till it was light."

Her father and mother looked puzzled.

If Ollie had been where she lay,

They knew he would surely have managed

To bring Sarah home in a day!

What "Ollie" was this that had guarded

Their daughter and kept her from fright?

They knew! And their hearts quaked in knowing—

A bear had been with her each night!

But Sarah, so young and so trusting,

Grew eager, the nearer they came,

To see once again her dear Ollie.

She ran to him, calling his name.

She suddenly stopped in amazement.

"Oh, Ollie! What happened to you?

You've grown, oh, so small! And, oh, Ollie,

You have a long tail, surely new!"

But Ollie, so fond of the infant,

    Now stiffened and sniffed her in fear.

The smell of the child told him surely

    A she-bear had often been near!

His hackles arose, and he started

    To growl at the smell he abhorred;

But Sarah moved quickly to hug him—

    Her Ollie, the dog she adored!

"Take care of her, Ollie," Pa ordered.

    And Ollie lay down on the ground

While Sarah crept closer to snuggle,

    Still needing her Ollie, though found.

The women had readied the pottage;

But no one, though hungry and weak,

Would venture to eat until Pa first

Had finished a blessing to speak.

Pa led them in singing "Old Hundred."

With earnest thanksgiving they sang.

And all through the mountains and forests,

The deep swelling melody rang:

"Praise God, from whom all blessings flow.

Praise Him, all creatures here below,

Praise Him above, ye heavenly host,

Praise Father, Son, and Holy Ghost!"

The angel of the LORD encampeth round about them that fear Him, and delivereth them.

Psalm 34:7